An Uncensored Guide to the Christmas Stories

This book explores the similarities and differences in the Bible's two Christmas stories as told by Matthew and Luke.

It retells the stories with cute, colorful and, sometimes, gory cartoons.

It then investigates many themes such as the prophecies the stories fulfill including the virgin birth, the birth in Bethlehem, going to Nazareth and the genealogies.

Here we go!

Overview of the Stories

Matthew's Christmas story is about kings, wise men and dreams. It involves a journey from Bethlehem to Egypt and then to Nazareth.

Luke's Christmas story is about priests, angels and shepherds. The journey begins in Nazareth, includes a trip to Bethlehem for a census and after visiting Jerusalem, they return to Nazareth.

What's the Same...

There are only a few basic ideas in the Christmas stories that Matthew and Luke agree on.

Prophesies fulfilled

- A **virgin** will give birth to the Messiah (Isaiah 7:14)

- The Messiah would come from **Bethlehem** in Judea (Micah 5:2, John 7:41-42)

- The Messiah would come from **Nazareth** in Galilee (Matthew 2:23)

- The Messiah would be a descendent of **Abraham** (Genesis 12:13)

- The Messiah would be a descendent of **King David** (2 Samuel 7:12-16, Psalm 89:3-4, Isaiah 9:7)

- The Messiah would be a descendent of the governor **Zerubbabel** and his father **Shealtiel** (Haggai 2:23)

Other similarities

- **Herod the Great** was ruling

- **Mary** was betrothed to marry **Joseph**

- An **angel** (or a dream about an angel) told someone about the pregnancy and instructed them to call their son **Jesus**

- They had **visitors** at night in **Bethlehem**

And that's about it!

Matthew and Luke flesh out the details in their own ways, each including many additional stories.

Matthew's Christmas Story: Kings, Wise Men & Dreams

The Virgin Mary was betrothed to marry Joseph, the carpenter. She conceived through the Holy Spirit. Joseph saw that Mary was pregnant and planned to separate privately.

An angel appeared to Joseph in a dream. It said to take Mary home as his wife and call the baby "Jesus".

So Joseph started to live with Mary as his wife, but did not have marital relations while she was pregnant.

Mary gave birth in Bethlehem and Joseph named the baby "Jesus".

Later, wise men from the east saw a special star rise, meaning the king of the Jews was born. They wanted to worship him so they travelled to Jerusalem in Judea to look for him.

The wise men's search for the new king of the Jews disturbed King Herod the Great and the rest of Jerusalem. Chief priests and teachers of the law said that according to a prophecy, the Messiah would be born in Bethlehem.

King Herod privately asked the wise men when the star had first appeared and to tell him when they had found the child in Bethlehem so that he too could worship the child.

The star the wise men had seen went ahead of them and stopped over the house where Jesus was.

In the house, the wise men met Mary and her child, Jesus. They bowed down and worshipped Jesus and gave him gifts.

The wise men were warned in their dreams not to go back to Herod, so they avoided Jerusalem on their trip home.

Then an angel appeared to Joseph in a dream. It told him to flee to Egypt because King Herod would try to kill the new king. So Joseph left with Mary and their child, Jesus, that night.

King Herod ordered all boys aged two years and younger living around Bethlehem to be killed.

After Herod died, an angel appeared to Joseph in a dream and told him to go back to Israel.

Joseph heard that Herod's son, Herod Archelaus, was ruling in Judea where Bethlehem was. He was warned in a dream to go to Nazareth in Galilee.

So Joseph, Mary and the child Jesus made their new home in Nazareth.

Luke's Christmas Story: Priests, Angels & Shepherds

Zacharias was a priest and the husband of Mary's relative Elizabeth.

One day, the angel Gabriel appeared to Zacharias to tell him his elderly wife would give birth to John the Baptist and that Zacharias would be unable to speak until the birth.

About six months later in Nazareth, the angel Gabriel appeared to Mary. It told her that she would give birth through the Holy Spirit and to name the baby "Jesus". The angel also told Mary about Elizabeth's pregnancy.

Mary then travelled to Zacharias and Elizabeth's house in the hill country of Judea. When Mary greeted her, Elizabeth's unborn baby leapt for joy.

Mary expressed a lengthy song, stayed with Elizabeth for about three months and returned home.

Soon, John the Baptist was born. On the eighth day, it was time to circumcise and name the baby. Zacharias wrote to call him John, and then his voice came back.

Zacharias was filled with the Holy Spirit and voiced a lengthy prophetic song.

Joseph and Mary had to travel to Bethlehem in Judea for a census because that was the hometown of Joseph's ancestor, King David.

Mary gave birth and laid the baby in an animal feeding trough, as there was no room in the inn.

That night, some shepherds were visited by an angel, who told them about the Messiah's birth. Then many more angels appeared, singing praises to God.

So the shepherds hurried off to Bethlehem and found Mary, Joseph and the baby. The shepherds told others about the angels then returned to the Messiah.

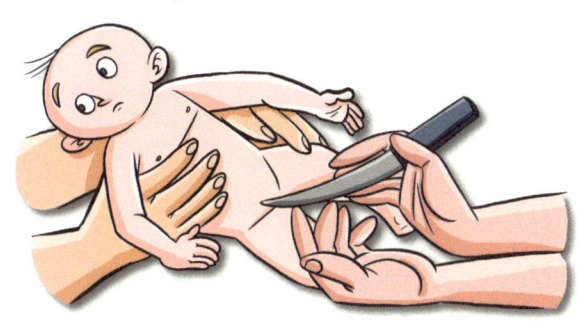

When the baby was eight days old, he was circumcised and given the name that the angel had given to Mary, "Jesus".

Weeks later, they went to the temple in Jerusalem to make Mary "clean" after her birth, by sacrificing a pair of doves.

After this, Joseph, Mary and their baby, Jesus, returned to their home in Nazareth.

13

The Virgin Mary

Prophesies fulfilled

- A virgin will give birth to the Messiah (Isaiah 7:14)

Mention of the virgin birth

The only books in the New Testament that clearly say that Jesus was born of a virgin, are Matthew and Luke. Matthew and Luke also have a lot of other unique stories in common and scholars believe they are based on a source they call "Q".

Some believe that Galatians 4:4 "...God sent out his Son, born to a woman..." means Paul thought that Jesus had a virgin mother. Matthew 11:11 uses the phrase "born to women", even though it is talking about John the Baptist, who had a human father. If Paul believed in the virgin birth, it would make sense that he would have mentioned it in Galatians.

Did Mary ever lose her virginity?

The Catholic and Orthodox churches teach that Mary never lost her virginity, but Matthew 1:25 implies Joseph had sex with her after Jesus was born.

According to Mark 6:3 and Matthew 13:55-56, Jesus had brothers and sisters. His brothers included James, Joses (or Joseph), Simon and Judas. It isn't clear whether they were children of Mary.

Mary in Islam

Like Luke, the Quran says that Mary was visited by the angel, Gabriel, and that Mary was a virgin.

Birth in Bethlehem, Growing up in Nazareth

Prophesies fulfilled

- The Messiah would come from **Bethlehem** in Judea (Micah 5:2, John 7:41-42)

- The Messiah would come from **Nazareth** in Galilee (Matthew 2:23)

- The Messiah would come from **Egypt** (Hosea 11:1) (only in Matthew)

John and Bethlehem

In John 7:41-42, people in a crowd say that Jesus isn't the Messiah because he comes from Galilee rather than Bethlehem. Those people also said that Jesus wasn't a descendent of King David. No one is said to correct them, nor does the author of John.

Some Christians argue that John knew that Jesus was from Bethlehem and that he was descended from King David and this could be an example of deliberate irony.

Ending up in Nazareth

In Luke, they had to go to the temple in Jerusalem within a few weeks of Jesus' birth and then they returned to Nazareth.

In Matthew, Herod had boys from the age of two and younger killed, so he believed Jesus would have been at least a year old. They stayed in Egypt until Herod died and only then did they travel to Nazareth.

Journeys in Matthew

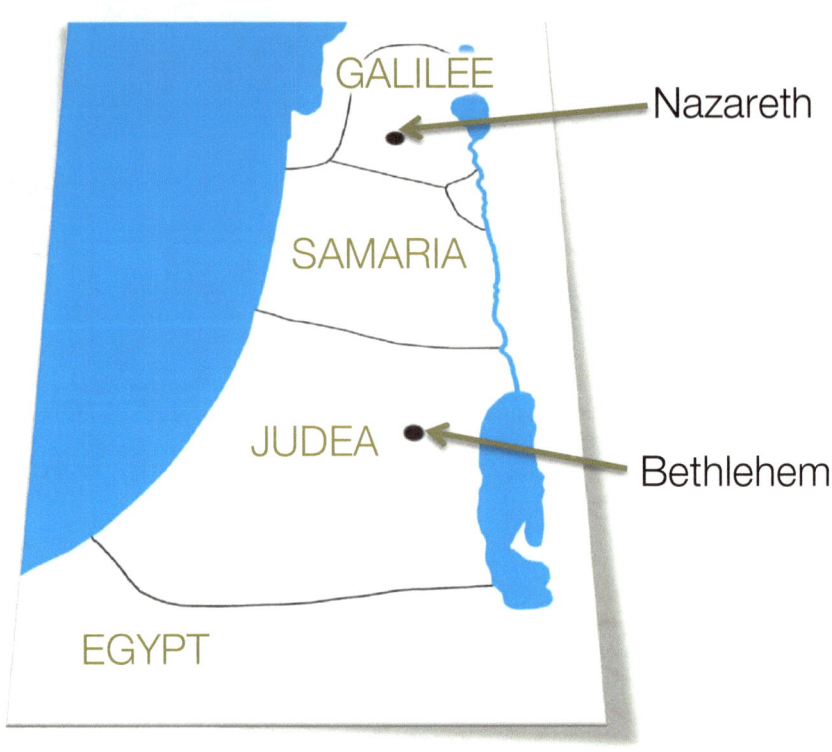

- **Bethlehem**
- **Egypt**
- **Nazareth**

In Matthew, their journey begins in Bethlehem, where they remain until the wise men arrive, after which they flee to Egypt. They stay in Egypt until Herod the Great dies. Rather than returning to Judea (where Bethlehem is), they move to Nazareth in Galilee. This is to avoid Herod the Great's son, Herod Archelaus, who was ruling Judea and Samaria. Their stay in Egypt is said to fulfill the prophecy "out of Egypt I called my son". Matthew focuses a lot on prophecies being fulfilled and only includes places that are linked to a prophecy (Bethlehem, Egypt and Nazareth).

Journeys in Luke

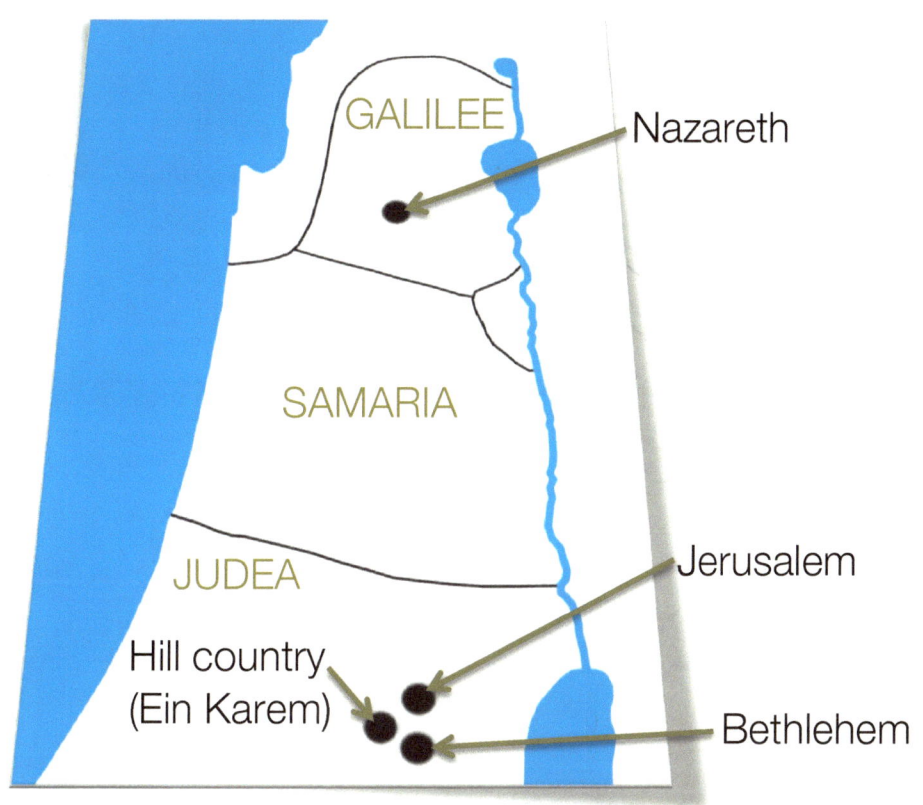

- **Nazareth**, Galilee
- Hill country, Judea
- **Nazareth**, Galilee
- Census in **Bethlehem**, Judea
- Jerusalem, Judea
- **Nazareth**, Galilee

In Luke, Mary and Joseph originally live in Nazareth. After an angel tells Mary about her relative, Elizabeth, being pregnant, she hurries over to her house in the hill country of Judea. This is about 80 miles from Nazareth, but only a few miles from Bethlehem and Jerusalem. After three months, Mary returns to Nazareth. Later, Mary and Joseph travel to Judea for a census in Bethlehem. In the following weeks, they travel to Jerusalem and then return to Nazareth.

The Genealogies

Prophesies fulfilled

- The Messiah would be a descendent of **Abraham** (Genesis 12:13)

- The Messiah would be a descendent of **King David** (2 Samuel 7:12-16, Psalm 89:3-4, Isaiah 9:7)

- The Messiah would be a descendent of the governor **Zerubbabel** and his father **Shealtiel** (Haggai 2:23)

Joseph and King David

In Matthew 1:16, 1:20 and Luke 1:27 and 3:23, Joseph is said to be a descendent of King David. This is shown in the genealogies in Matthew and Luke. While they agree about the ancestors of David, they almost entirely disagree about the ancestors of Joseph after David. The exception to this is that both mention Zerubbabel, a governor who rebuilt the temple in Jerusalem, and his father Shealtiel. They disagree on who Shealtiel's father was, though they agree that he is a descendent of David.

Why are the genealogies different?

The earliest tradition that explained the differences in the genealogies involved the concept of levirate marriage. This idea was mentioned in the 3rd century AD by Sextus Julius Africanus in "Epistle to Aristides". In that version, Matthew talked about Joseph's natural father while Luke talked about Joseph's legal father.

Centuries later, John of Damascus, who lived from 675 – 749 AD, was unhappy with that explanation and argued that the genealogy in Luke was actually showing that Mary was descended from David.
Though the Bible doesn't suggest that Mary is a descendent of David, Luke says that her relative, Elizabeth, is a descendent of Moses' brother, Aaron (who isn't an ancestor of David). Despite this, the idea that Mary was a descendent of David is the most popular explanation today amongst Christians.

Another possibility is that at least one of the genealogies isn't accurate and may even have been deliberately invented.

Matthew	Luke
	Adam - Terah
Abraham	**Abraham**
Issac – Jesse	Issac – Jesse
David	**David**
Solomon	Nathan
Rehoboam	Mattatha
Abijah	Menan
Asa	Melea
Jehoshaphat	Eliakim
Joram	Jonan
Uzziah	Joseph
Jotham	Judah
Ahaz	Simeon
Hezekiah	Levi
Manasseh	Matthat
Amon	Jorim
Josiah	Eliezer
Jechoniah	Jose
	Er
	Elmodam
	Cosam
	Addi
	Melchi
	Neri
Shealtiel	**Shealtiel**
Zerubbabel	**Zerubbabel**
Abiud	Rhesa
Eliakim	Joanan
Azor	Judah
Zadok	Joseph
Achim	Semein
Eliud	Mattathias
Eleazar	Maath
Matthan	Naggai
Jacob	Esli
Joseph	Nahum
	Amos
	Mattathias
	Joseph
	Jannai
	Melchi
	Levi
	Matthat
	Heli
	Joseph
Jesus	**Jesus**

The Lengthy Songs of Elizabeth, Mary & Zacharias

Elizabeth's and Mary's songs
Luke 1:41-55

When Elizabeth heard Mary's greeting, the baby leaped in her womb, and Elizabeth was filled with the Holy Spirit. She called out with a loud voice, and said,

> "Blessed are you among women, and blessed is the fruit of your womb! Why am I so favored, that the mother of my Lord should come to me?
> For behold, when the voice of your greeting came into my ears, the baby leaped in my womb for joy!
> Blessed is she who believed, for there will be a fulfillment of the things which have been spoken to her from the Lord!"

Mary's relative, Elizabeth

Mary being related to Elizabeth (Luke 1:36) means that Jesus was related to Elizabeth's son, John the Baptist. Mary also lived with Elizabeth for three months. Even though all four gospels and Acts talk about John the Baptist and most talk about Mary, only Luke talks about this interesting connection between Jesus and John the Baptist.

Mary said,
> "My soul magnifies the Lord.
> My spirit has rejoiced in God my Savior,
> for he has looked at the humble state of his servant.
> For behold, from now on, all generations will call me blessed.
> For he who is mighty has done great things for me.
> Holy is his name.
> His mercy is for generations of generations on those who fear him.
> He has shown strength with his arm.
> He has scattered the proud in the imagination of their hearts.
> He has put down princes from their thrones.
> And has exalted the lowly.
> He has filled the hungry with good things.
> He has sent the rich away empty.
> He has given help to Israel, his servant, that he might remember mercy,
> As he spoke to our fathers,
> to Abraham and his offspring forever."

Zacharias' song – After his son, John the Baptist was born
Luke 1:67-79

His father, Zacharias, was filled with the Holy Spirit, and prophesied, saying,
> "Blessed be the Lord, the God of Israel,
> for he has visited and redeemed his people;
> and has raised up a horn of salvation for us in the house of his servant David
> (as he spoke by the mouth of his holy prophets who have been from of old),
> salvation from our enemies, and from the hand of all who hate us;
> to show mercy towards our fathers,
> to remember his holy covenant,
> the oath which he spoke to Abraham, our father,
> to grant to us that we, being delivered out of the hand of our enemies,
> should serve him without fear,
> In holiness and righteousness before him all the days of our life.
> And you, child, will be called a prophet of the Most High,
> for you will go before the face of the Lord to prepare his ways,
> to give knowledge of salvation to his people by the remission of their sins,
> because of the tender mercy of our God,
> whereby the dawn from on high will visit us,
> to shine on those who sit in darkness and the shadow of death;
> to guide our feet into the way of peace."

Were the songs passed down accurately?

The lengthy songs of Zacharias and Mary were allegedly spoken thirty years before Jesus' ministry, passed along by word-of-mouth and only carefully written down in Greek decades later.

However, the simple fact that Jesus was born in Bethlehem wasn't known by the crowd in John 7:41-42.

Zacharias' song was spoken when neither Mary nor Joseph was around. How did the words of his song get passed down to the author of Luke?

When Was Jesus Born?

When Herod the Great was alive

Jesus was alive when King Herod the Great was alive, but most scholars believe that Herod died in 4 BC, so Jesus must have been born in 4 BC or earlier.

December 25th

Christmas was first celebrated on December the 25th in the year 336 AD when the first Christian Roman Emperor, Constantine, was ruling. The date was chosen because pagan festivals celebrating the sun were already observed then.

During the census

The census that Joseph and Mary travelled to Bethlehem for was when Quirinius was governor of Syria. The ancient historian, Flavius Josephus, who also mentions Jesus and John the Baptist, states that this census occurred 37 years after the battle of Actium. This occurred in September 31 BC, which means that the census, when Jesus was born in Luke, would have happened in 6 or 7 AD.

Ruling Herods

King Herod the Great

In Matthew, Herod the Great ordered boys aged two years old and younger around Bethlehem to be killed in an attempt to kill the new king of the Jews. He also had one of his many wives and three of his sons executed after putting them on trial for treason.

Herod the Great in Luke

Even though Matthew says that Joseph and his family fled to Egypt to avoid Herod's massacre, in Luke, Herod is only mentioned when introducing the priest, Zacharias.

Herod Archelaus

After Herod the Great died at the age of 69, his kingdom was split up amongst three of his sons. Archelaus ruled over Judea and, in Matthew, he was the reason why Joseph didn't return to Bethlehem. Instead, Joseph made a home in Nazareth in Galilee.

Herod Antipas

This Herod ruled Galilee and offered his step-daughter anything she wanted, even half of his kingdom. She asked for the head of John the Baptist on a platter, which he gave her. In Luke 23, Pilate sends Jesus to Herod; after Jesus wouldn't perform a miracle for Herod or answer his questions, Herod and his soldiers mock Jesus and send him back to Pilate.

Lowly vs Regal Beginnings

Lowly Luke

Though in Luke, angels were seen by Zacharias, Mary and the shepherds, Jesus had pretty humble beginnings.

After his birth, Jesus was laid in a feeding trough. He was visited by shepherds who "saw" him. The shepherds told others about Jesus, who were amazed, but the others didn't seek out Jesus. When the shepherds returned, they glorified and praised God rather than worshipping the baby.

Leviticus 12 instructed mothers who had recently given birth to sacrifice a lamb as a burnt offering. It says that if she can't afford a lamb, then she should use a dove or small pigeon for the burnt sacrifice. This is what Mary did (Luke 2:24), suggesting she must not have had enough money to buy a lamb.

The king of the Jews in Matthew

In Matthew, a star in the heavens announced that the king of the Jews was born. It caused wise men from far away to come and worship Jesus and give him lavish gifts. In Matthew, Jesus was living in a house rather than being in a manger (Matthew 2:11). King Herod felt so threatened by Jesus that he attempted to kill him.

Were the wise men kings?

Though Matthew doesn't say that the wise men were kings, there are Old Testament passages that many believe prophesy that the Messiah would be worshipped and given gifts by kings (Psalm 68:29, 72:10-11, Isaiah 49:7, 60:3-6).

Jesus as the Messiah

In the Christmas stories

In the Christmas stories, there are many things pointing to Jesus being the Messiah such as an angel appearing to Mary, her virgin birth, the angels appearing to the shepherds and the star that appeared to the wise men who wanted to worship this new king.

Also, Luke 2:25-35 talks about Simeon, who recognized the baby Jesus as the Messiah.

The secret Messiah

After that, there is no mention of Jesus being the Messiah until he is about thirty (Luke 3:23). Early on, Jesus didn't want his disciples to tell others about him being the Messiah (Matthew 16:20, Mark 8:29-30, Luke 9:20-21). Jesus also stopped demons from speaking to prevent them from telling people that he was the Messiah (Luke 4:41).

The crowd's knowledge of the Christmas stories

At a festival in Jerusalem, which Jesus' brothers also attended (John 7:10), some of the crowd said that Jesus was the Messiah (John 7:41-42). No-one brought up the Christmas stories that allegedly took place thirty years earlier. There was no mention of a virgin birth, angels or wise men following a star being used as evidence that Jesus was the Messiah. Some of the crowd were aware of the prophecy that the Messiah would come from Bethlehem and they were sure that that didn't apply to Jesus.

Why Were Things Left Out?

Some things Matthew didn't mention

- Elizabeth and Zacharias, including Mary's three month stay with them in the hill country of Judea

- The angel appearing to Mary and her song

- Travelling to Bethlehem because of a census

- Having no room in the inn and Jesus being laid in a manger (instead he was in a house)

- The shepherds

- Going to the temple in Jerusalem

- That Nazareth was their "own town"

Some things Luke didn't mention

- An angel in a dream telling Joseph about Mary's pregnancy

- The wise men or the star

- Going to Egypt

- Herod ordering boys two years old and younger to be killed

- Deciding to go to Nazareth to avoid Herod's son in Judea

Things other books didn't mention

- Jesus was born of a virgin

- Jesus was born in Bethlehem (John 7:41-42)

Were the authors unaware of things?

One explanation for these things being left out is that the authors of the gospels were unaware of them. Mary and Joseph would have known about most of them, but perhaps the people they passed the stories down to only heard or remembered some of them. So some people only knew about an angel appearing in dreams to Joseph, while others only knew about an angel appearing to Mary.

Did they decide not to include things?

Another explanation is that Matthew and Luke decided not to include certain stories. Maybe Matthew wanted to focus on angels in dreams, kings and prophecy fulfillment (like the trip to Egypt) while Luke wanted to focus on real life angels and Jesus' humble beginnings in a manger being visited by shepherds.

Were some things not factual?

The Messiah had to fulfill prophecies; perhaps some of these fulfillments were invented or based on rumors during the time these books were written. That would explain why Matthew and Luke fulfill the prophecies in different ways – with different genealogies and different stories involving Bethlehem and Nazareth.

There are additional stories about Mary and Joseph in writings that aren't official parts of the Bible including the Infancy Gospel of James, which says that Mary rode a donkey to get to Bethlehem. These apocryphal writings aren't usually considered factual.

Conclusion

In the end, your explanations for why the Christmas stories are so different depend on how trustworthy you believe the Bible is. If you are committed to believing that every word of the Bible is true, then the differences must all be explained by the authors not being aware of things or deciding not to include them. It also means having to explain the apparent contradictions in the genealogies and journeys. Often, Christians say that in Luke, Mary was a descendent of David, even though John of Damascus only came up with this theory centuries after Jesus' birth.

An alternative is that the stories are so different because they are based on independent rumors or fiction, intended to show that the Messiah's prophecies were fulfilled. They could involve parables that utilize symbolism to tell deeper "truths". Furthermore, some people believe that some stories in Matthew are based on Old Testament stories.

There is also another possibility – you might be open-minded that the Bible might not be factual, but despite the problems in the journeys and genealogies, you come to the conclusion that it is all factual and can all be reconciled to real history.

©2017 Lucas Walker. All rights reserved.

lucas@sky-walker.net

Scripture taken from the World English Bible.

First Edition

ISBN 978-0648232209

www.ingramcontent.com/pod-product-compliance
Lightning Source LLC
Chambersburg PA
CBHW042145290426
44110CB00002B/114